CONTENTS

What are oranges?   4

Kinds of oranges   6

In the past   8

Around the world   10

Looking at oranges   12

Picking oranges   14

Checking and washing   16

Waxing and sorting   18

Labels and packing   20

Eating oranges   22

Good for you   24

Healthy eating   26

Orange smoothie recipe   28

Glossary   30

More books to read   32

Index   32

Words written in bold, **like this**, are explained in the Glossary.

WHAT ARE ORANGES?

Oranges are a kind of **citrus fruit**. Lemons and limes are citrus fruits too. People eat more oranges than any other citrus fruit in the world.

Food
ORANGES

Louise Spilsbury

www.heinemann.co.uk/library
Visit our website to find out more information about Heinemann Library books.

To order:
 Phone 44 (0) 1865 888066
 Send a fax to 44 (0) 1865 314091
 Visit the Heinemann Bookshop at www.heinemann.co.uk/library to browse our catalogue and order online.

First published in Great Britain by Heinemann Library,
Halley Court, Jordan Hill, Oxford OX2 8EJ
a division of Reed Educational and Professional Publishing Ltd.
Heinemann is a registered trademark of Reed Educational and Professional Publishing Ltd.

OXFORD MELBOURNE AUCKLAND
JOHANNESBURG BLANTYRE GABORONE
IBADAN PORTSMOUTH (NH) USA CHICAGO

Designed by Celia Floyd
Illustrated by Alan Fraser and Jeff Edwards
Originated by Ambassador Litho Ltd
Printed in Hong Kong/China by South China Printing Co.

ISBN 0 431 12772 7 (hardback)   ISBN 0 431 12777 8 (paperback)
06 05 04 03 02   06 05 04 03
10 9 8 7 6 5 4 3 2   10 9 8 7 6 5 4 3 2 1

British Library Cataloguing in Publication Data
Spilsbury, Louise
  Oranges. – (Food)
  1. Oranges 2. Juvenile literature
  I. Title
  641.3'431

Acknowledgements
The Publishers would like to thank the following for permission to reproduce photographs:
Corbis: pp.5, 7, 8, 12, 16, 9; Holt Studios International: pp.11, 14, 17; Liz Eddison: pp.4, 23, 28, 29 (top and bottom); Richard Spilsbury: p.24; Photodisc: p.13; Pictor International: p.15; Sequoia: pp.18, 19, 20, 21; Stone: p.25; Telegraph Colour Library: p.22; Visuals Unlimited: Eric Anderson, p.6.

Cover photograph reproduced with permission of Gareth Boden.

Every effort has been made to contact copyright holders of any material reproduced in this book.
Any omissions will be rectified in subsequent printings if notice is given to the Publishers.

Oranges, like other citrus fruits, grow on trees. A group of orange trees growing together is called a **grove**. This orange grove is in the USA.

KINDS OF ORANGES

Navel, Valencia and blood oranges
are sweet oranges. We take the **peel**
off sweet oranges and eat the fruit
inside **raw**.

Valencia orange   blood orange   Navel orange

Seville oranges are **sour**. They are not sweet so we do not eat them raw. People cook them with sugar to make **marmalade**.

IN THE PAST

The first orange trees grew in Asia. Alexander the Great was a Greek king. His army travelled far. He brought oranges from Asia to Europe over 2000 years ago.

Christopher Columbus was the first person from Europe to go to America. In 1493 he planted **seeds** to grow the first orange trees there.

AROUND THE WORLD

This map of the world shows the places that grow most oranges today. Oranges grow best where it is very hot in summer and chilly in winter.

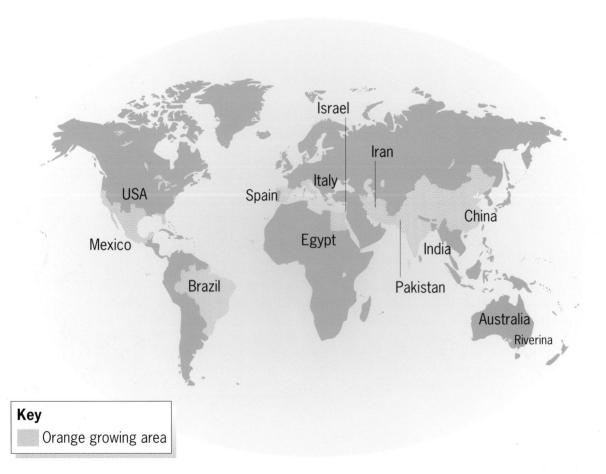

Israel

Iran

Italy

USA

Spain

China

Mexico

Egypt

India

Brazil

Pakistan

Australia

Riverina

Key
Orange growing area

Oranges also need plenty of water to grow well. In countries where there is not enough rain, **irrigation channels** give the trees the water they need.

LOOKING AT ORANGES

Orange trees have shiny green leaves and white flowers. They grow on branches from a tall **trunk**. The tree's **roots** are underground.

leaves

branch

trunk

roots
(underground)

Most oranges are round and have a thick orange-coloured **peel**. The peel protects the **flesh** inside. The white bits are called **pith**. Some oranges have pips (**seeds**).

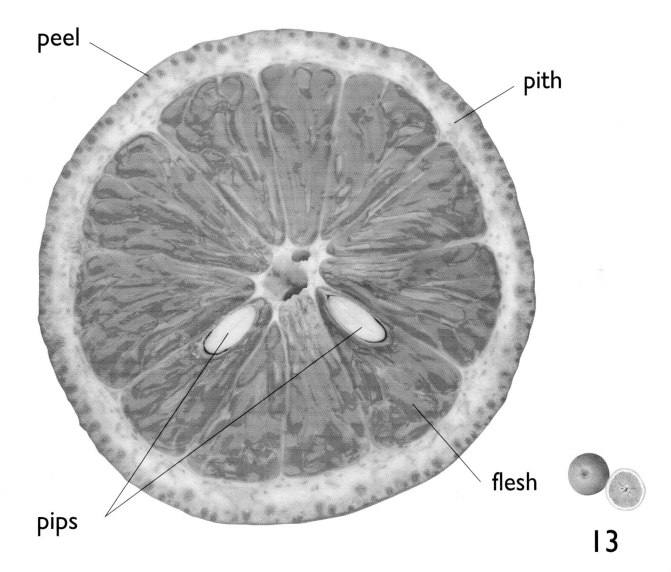

peel

pith

pips

flesh

PICKING ORANGES

Most orange trees grow flowers in spring. After a while the flowers die and drop off. Oranges grow in place of some of the flowers.

The oranges grow on the trees until they are **ripe** (ready to eat). Workers pick the ripe oranges by hand. They are careful not to damage the fruits.

CHECKING AND WASHING

Workers put the oranges into big tubs. A machine lifts the tubs and tips the oranges into trailers. These take the oranges to a **packing house**.

At the packing house workers check the oranges. They throw away bad or damaged ones. A machine washes the fruit to get rid of dust and dirt.

WAXING AND SORTING

Oranges are covered with a very thin layer of natural **wax**. Washing rubs this off. Machines put a new layer on. This helps to keep the oranges fresh.

Next, the oranges are sorted by size. A camera takes pictures to see how big they are. Then the oranges are sorted into different sizes.

LABELS AND PACKING

Another machine puts a little sticker onto every orange. The sticker tells you what sort of orange it is and where it comes from.

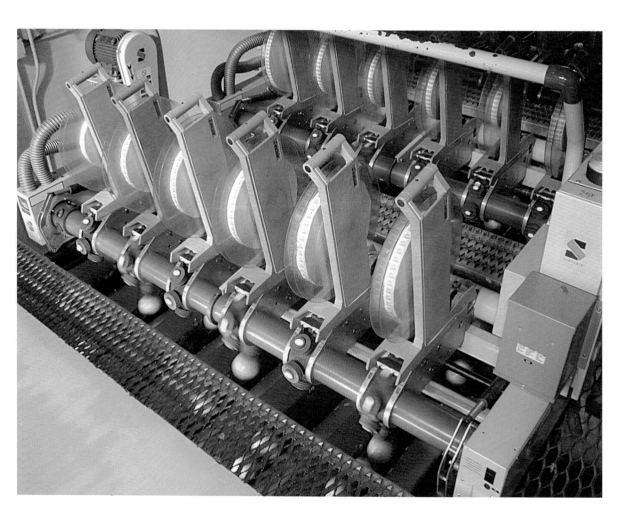

Packing machines put the oranges into boxes. Some oranges are sold in the country where they grew. Others are **exported** (sold to other countries).

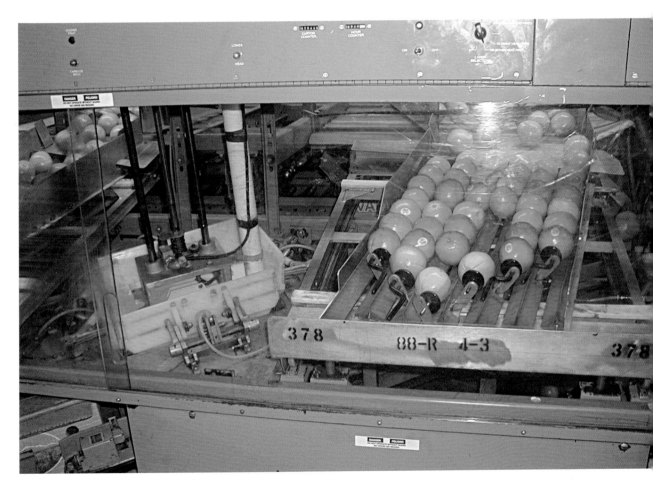

EATING ORANGES

Many oranges are made into orange juice. In a **factory**, machines squeeze the oranges to get the juice out. Then they put it into cartons or bottles.

Oranges are used to make
marmalade to spread on toast.
Oranges are also used to flavour
cakes and muffins, and other foods.

GOOD FOR YOU

Oranges are rich in **vitamins**.
Vitamins help your body to grow and
they protect you from illness.

Oranges also contain **fibre**. Fibre is a part of some foods that passes through your body when you eat it. It helps keep your body healthy.

HEALTHY EATING

You need to eat different kinds of food to keep you well. This food pyramid shows you how much of each different food you need.

You should eat some of the things at the bottom and in the middle of the pyramid every day. Sweet foods are at the top of the pyramid. Try not to eat too many of these!

The food in each part of the pyramid helps your body in different ways.

Oranges belong in the middle of the pyramid.

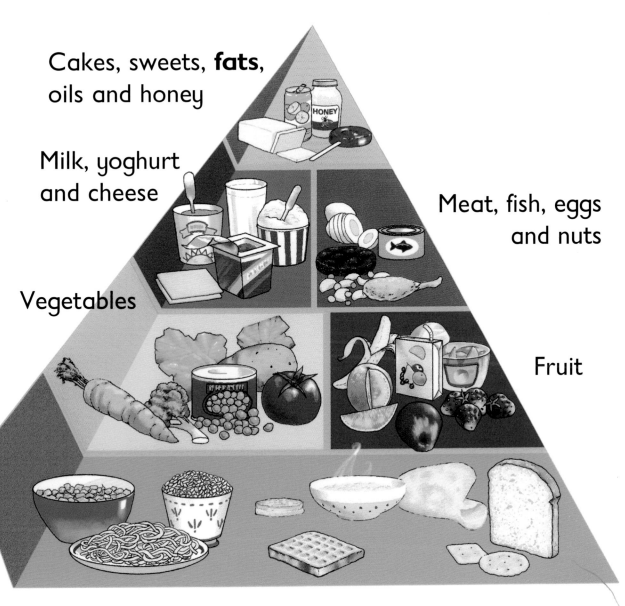

Cakes, sweets, **fats**, oils and honey

Milk, yoghurt and cheese

Meat, fish, eggs and nuts

Vegetables

Fruit

Bread, **cereals**, rice and pasta

ORANGE SMOOTHIE RECIPE

1 Peel the bananas and cut it into pieces.

2 Chop the strawberries into pieces.

Ask an adult to help you!

You will need:
- 1 cup of orange juice
- 1 cup of fresh or frozen strawberries
- 2 fresh bananas

3 Pour the orange juice into a blender.

4 Add the strawberries and bananas. Ask an adult to blend them until smooth.

5 Pour the smoothie into two tall glasses. Decorate with an orange slice and a strawberry, if you like.

GLOSSARY

cereals   grains like wheat and rice that are used to make flour, bread and breakfast foods

citrus fruit   kind of fruit that grows on citrus trees. Citrus fruits have thick peel, pulpy flesh and you can eat them. Oranges, limes, lemons and grapefruits are citrus fruits.

exported   when food or other goods are taken from one country to be sold in another country

factory   large building where things are made, such as toys or shoes, or food and drinks

fats   type of food. Butter, oil and margarine are kinds of fat.

fibre   part of a plant that passes through our bodies when we eat it

flesh   part of some fruits that we can eat. The flesh is inside the peel or rind.

grove   piece of land where orange trees are grown. They are often planted in rows.

irrigation channels   passages that a farmer creates to get water from one place to another. They supply water to the groves. This water helps the oranges trees to grow.

marmalade   kind of jam made from oranges and sugar

packing house   building where fruit or other goods are sorted and packed. Then they are ready to be taken to the shops to be sold.

peel   skin or rind of a fruit like an orange

pith   white bits in a fruit like an orange

raw   not cooked

ripe   when a fruit is ready to eat

roots   part of a plant under the ground. Roots hold the plant firmly in the ground. They also take in water from the soil for the plant.

seeds   made by flowers. They are released from a plant and grow into a new plant.

sour   not sweet

trunk   stem of a tree. Trunks hold up the branches with their leaves and flowers to get the warmth and light the tree needs to grow.

vitamins   food contains vitamins. Vitamins help us grow and protect our bodies from illness.

wax   fatty stuff made by some plants and animals. You cannot see the layer of wax on oranges, but it helps to stop the fruit drying out.

MORE BOOKS TO READ

Plants: Flowers, Fruits and Seeds, Angela Royston, Heinemann Library, 1999

Safe and Sound: Eat Well, Angela Royston, Heinemann Library, 1999

Senses: Tasting, Karen Hartley, Chris Macro, Phillip Taylor, Heinemann Library, 2000

The Senses: Taste, Mandy Suhr, Hodder Wayland, 1994

INDEX

Alexander the Great   8

Christopher Columbus   9

citrus fruit   4, 5, 30

exports   21, 30

factory   22, 30

fibre   25, 30

flesh   13, 30

food pyramid   26–27

groves   5, 30

irrigation   11, 30

lemons   4

limes   4

marmalade   7, 23, 31

orange juice   22

packing house   16, 17, 31

peel   6, 13, 31

pith   13, 31

seeds   9, 13, 31

vitamins   24, 31

wax   18, 31